BRANCH LINES TO PEMBROKE AND CARDIGAN

Vic Mitchell and Keith Smith

MP Middleton Press

Cover pictures:

Front: A local train from Whitland arrives at Tenby behind 2-6-2T no. 4569 in August 1962. Two camping coaches could usually be found in the siding in the Summer. (Colour-Rail.com)

Back upper: Recorded at Llanglydwen on 25th June 1962 was 2-6-2T no. 5550. This was the last year of operation of passenger trains on the Cardigan branch. (Colour-Rail.com)

Back lower: A Swindon built class 120 DMU waits in the bay platform at Whitland before a trip on the Pembroke branch on 27th September 1982. (P.Jones)

Published September 2012

ISBN 978 1 908174 29 1

© Middleton Press, 2012

Design Deborah Esher

Published by
  Middleton Press
  Easebourne Lane
  Midhurst
  West Sussex
  GU29 9AZ
Tel: 01730 813169
Fax: 01730 812601
Email: info@middletonpress.co.uk
www.middletonpress.co.uk

Printed in the United Kingdom by Henry Ling Limited, at the Dorset Press, Dorchester, DT1 1HD

CONTENTS

INDEX

ACKNOWLEDGEMENTS

We are very grateful for the assistance received from many of those mentioned in the credits also to B. Bennett, A.R.Carder, G.Croughton, P.Gilson, S.C.Jenkins, P.J.Kelley, N.Langridge, B.Lewis, D.T.Rowe, Mr D. and Dr S.Salter, G.T.V.Stacey, S.Vincent, T.Walsh and in particular, our always supportive wives, Barbara Mitchell and Janet Smith.

I. Route map for the early 1960s. (Railway Magazine)

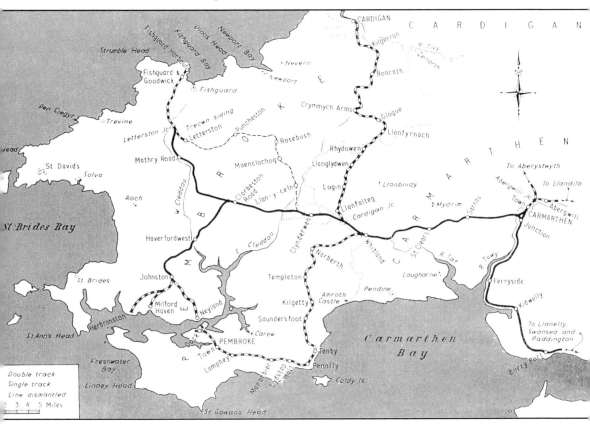

GEOGRAPHICAL SETTING

Pembroke Branch

The route runs west from Whitland along the Lampeter Vale, close to the east flowing Afon Marlais. Having climbed to Narbeth, it turns south to climb over a series of east-west ridges. Red sandstone is followed by limestone and then millstone grit, in quick succession. There follows a journey of about five miles over once-productive coal measures, centred on Saundersfoot.

Further millstone grit is crossed to reach the popular holiday resort of Tenby, which overlooks Carmarthen Bay. Soon turning west, the route follows the same outcrop most of the way to the important port of Pembroke. For many generations, there was a dockyard for the Royal Navy here, but more recently, it has become a terminal point for Irish car ferries. It also has a ferry service to Neyland, across the east end of Milford Haven.

The branch was built in Pembrokeshire, except for a mile at its east end. The county had an invisible boundary, called the Landsker, between its Welsh inclined communities to the north and the English ones to the south. In recent generations, this has been represented by the main line. The place names and some of the architecture still reflect these differences.

The county became part of Dyfed in 1975, but was restored within its old boundaries in 1996. The same happened to Cardiganshire, but its name was changed to Ceredigion, an earlier title.

Cardigan Branch

After leaving the main line, the single track climbs up the steep sided valley of the Afon Taf to Crymmych Arms. Nearby is the summit, at nearly 800ft above sea level. An almost continuous descent follows to enter the valley of the Afon Teifi, on which the county town of Cardigan is situated, about three miles from its mouth. The branch was almost entirely in Pembrokeshire and on rocks of minor commercial importance. However, there was some lead and silver mining, plus limited slate slab production.

The southern six miles were in Carmarthenshire and the northern half mile in Cardiganshire. The maps are to the scale of 25ins to 1 mile, with north at the top unless otherwise indicated. Furthermore as Welsh spelling and hyphenation has varied over the years we have generally used the form of the period.

Gradient Profile for the Pembroke branch.

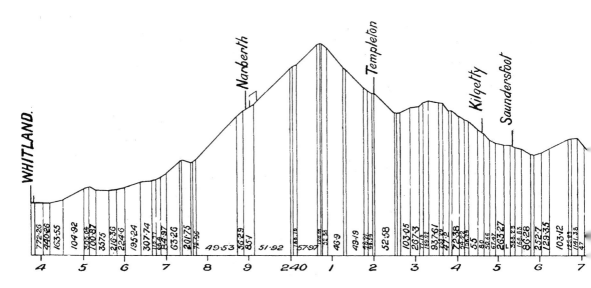

HISTORICAL BACKGROUND

The South Wales Railway opened between Carmarthen and Haverfordwest on 2nd January 1854, the track being broad gauge (7ft 0¼ins). It became part of the Great Western Railway in 1862 and was converted to standard gauge in May 1872.

The Pembroke & Tenby Railway received its Act on 21st July 1859 and a standard gauge single line came into use between the two towns on 24th July 1863. The extension to Pembroke Dock was opened on 8th August 1864 and trains were operated by the contractors, Davies & Roberts.

The line from a new station at Tenby through to the GWR at Whitland came into use on 4th September 1866. Goods lines in Pembroke opened to the Dockyard in 1871 and to Hobbs Point Pier in 1872. The branch became part of the GWR in 1897 and contractor operation ceased then.

The Cardigan branch was created by the Whitland & Taf Vale Railway under an Act of 1869. It opened on 24th March 1873, for freight only, from Whitland to Glogue. Extension to Crymmych Arms followed in the Summer and passengers were carried thus far from 12th July 1875, although without official approval. Light railway rules applied and the limited rolling stock was very busy.

A Bill in February 1877 allowed extension to Cardigan and this opened on 31st August 1886, when the GWR took over operation of the entire branch. It acquired the line in 1890 and became the Western Region of British Railways upon nationalisation in 1948. Passenger service ceased on 10th September 1962 and goods traffic ended on 27th May 1963. Its withdrawal on the Pembroke Branch is detailed later.

Privatisation in 1996 resulted in South Wales & West providing services to Pembroke ("South" was dropped in 1998). However, after reorganisation in 2001, Wales & Borders became the franchisee. Arriva Trains Wales took over in December 2003. London services were provided by Great Western Trains from 4th February 1996, this changing to First Great Western on 1st April 2006.

Station closures and freight withdrawals are given in the captions.

July 1927

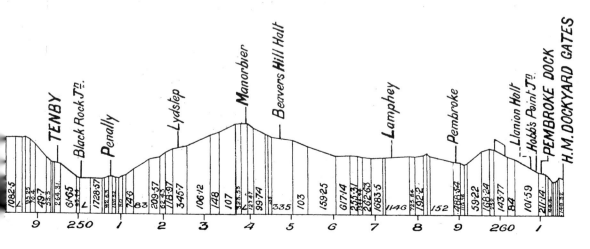

PASSENGER SERVICES

Pembroke Branch

The initial service on the P&TR comprised three trains, weekdays only. This was increased to five for the final months of 1863, but it reverted to three in the next year. One of the broad gauge tracks from Carmarthen was provided with a third rail to enable branch trains to start there.

The table below indicates down train frequency in sample years, but excludes those running on less than four days per week.

	Weekdays	Sundays
1869	5	1
1887	7	1
1907	6	1
1927	7	3
1947	5	1
1962	8	1
1987	8	3
2007	9	3

Through trains from London have operated since the 1870s, with up to four per weekday and one on Sundays for much of the 1930s, 1950s and 1960s. There was still one on mid-Summer Saturdays in 2012.

Pembroke's former Naval Dock was used by B&I from 21st May 1979 for their ferries to Cork and from May 1980 to Rosslare. The Cork trips ceased on 2nd February 1983, although a bus link had been provided from the station, with an enhanced rail service as well.

Cardigan Branch

For most of the operation in the 19th century, three trains were provided on weekdays, this increasing to four until closure. No Sunday trains have been found.

The final timetables showed "Halt" applied to five names, following withdrawal of staff. However, the suffix did not appear on the stations and so is not used herein.

Gradient Profile for the Cardigan branch.

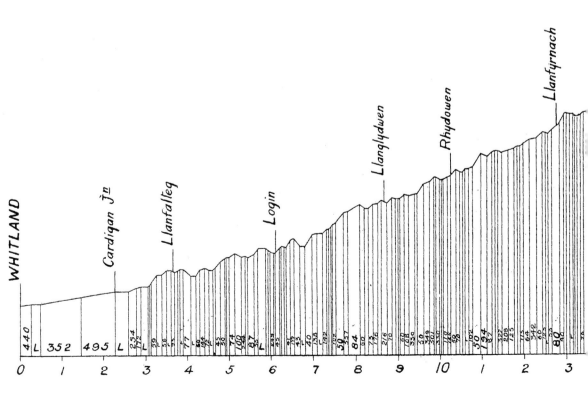

WHITLAND, TENBY and PEMBROKE DOCK

Miles		Week Days pm	am	am	am Y	am Y	am Y	pm T	pm	Sundays pm Y
	104London (Pad.) dep	9P25	1 0	..	8 55	10 55	11 55	1 55	3R55	2 55
—	**Whitland** dep	6a 5	9 50	10 45	2p58	4p15	5p59	8 34	10 0	9 50
5¼	Narberth	6 16	10 0	10 55	3 10	4 25	6 12	8 45	1010	10 0
8¼	Templeton	6 25	1010	11 4	3 19	4 35	6 21	8 55	1020	10 10
10¾	Kilgetty	6 31	1015	11 10	3 25	4 40	6 27	9 1	1027	10 16
11½	Saundersfoot	6 34	1020	11 15	3 29	4 45	6 32	9 5	1030	10 20
15¾	**Tenby** arr	**6 42**	**1030**	**11 24**	**3 39**	**4 57**	**6 40**	**9 13**	**1039**	**10 28**
	dep	**6 47**	**1033**	**11 28**	**3 42**	**5 0**	**6 47**	**9 16**	**1040**	**10 30**
17	Penally	6 51	1036	11 32	3 46	5 3	6 50	9 20	1045	10 35
20¼	Manorbier	6 59	1048	11 44	3 54	5 10	6 59	9 30	1053	10 44
21	Beavers Hill Halt	..	..	11F47	..	..	..	..	D	..
23¾	Lamphey	7 5	1055	11 50	4 0	5 16	7 4	9 36	11 0	10 50
25¼	Pembroke	7 10	1058	11 56	4 6	5 20	7 9	9 40	11 5	10 56
27¼	**Pembroke Dock** arr	**7 15**	**11 5**	**12 1**	**4 17**	**5 26**	**7 15**	**9 50**	**1110**	**11 2**

Miles		Week Days am Y	am Y	am T	pm Y	pm	pm	pm	Sundays am A	pm
—	**Pembroke Dock** dep	**7 30**	**1030**	**1125**	**1 5**	**3 50**	**6 15**	**8 0**	**1155**	**5 55**
2	Pembroke	7 35	1035	1130	1 10	3 55	6 20	8 7	12 0	6 0
3½	Lamphey	7 40	1040	1135	1 15	4 8	6 25	8 10	12 5	6 5
6¾	Beavers Hill Halt	..	..	..	..	4 13	..	..	..	..
7	Manorbier	7 50	1048	1144	1 25	4 20	6 34	8 19	1213	6 14
10½	Penally	7 55	1055	1153	1 32	4 26	6 40	8 25	1220	6 20
11½	**Tenby** arr	**8 0**	**11 0**	**1158**	**1 36**	**4 32**	**6 43**	**8 28**	**1225**	**6 23**
	dep	**8 3**	**11 3**	**12 0**	**1 40**	**4 34**	**6 50**	**8 30**	**1228**	**6 25**
15¾	Saundersfoot	8 14	1117	1212	1 50	4 45	7 0	8 41	1239	6 35
16½	Kilgetty	8 18	1120	1217	1 55	4 50	7 7	8 45	1243	6 40
19	Templeton	8 25	1128	1224	2 0	4 57	7 13	8 58	1250	6 47
22	Narberth	8 34	1137	1233	2 10	5 6	7 22	9 8	1259	6 55
27¼	**Whitland** arr	**8 45**	**1147**	**1245**	**2 22**	**5 16**	**7 33**	**9 18**	**1 8**	**7 6**
261	104London (Pad.) arr	3 10	6 2	7 10	7 45	..	4a40	..	8 15	4a30

A Runs 17th and 24th September, 1961 and commencing 20th May, 1962 Note "Y" applies
a am
D Calls on Wednesdays and Saturdays to set down
F Fridays only

P Sunday to Friday nights inclusive
p pm
R Restaurant Car Paddington to Swansea
T Through Carriages between Paddington and Pembroke Dock. Buffet Car between Paddington and Swansea.

Y Through Carriages between Paddington and Pembroke Dock Restaurant Car between Paddington and Swansea

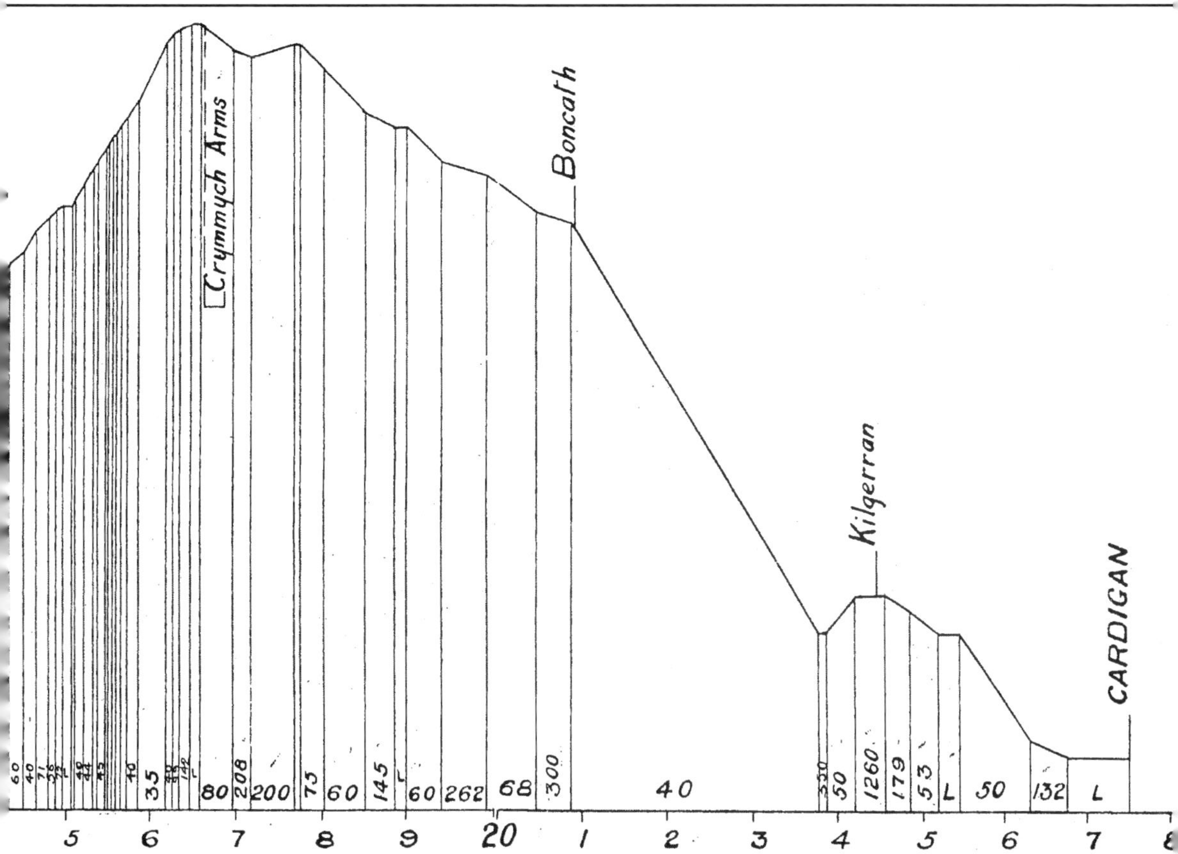

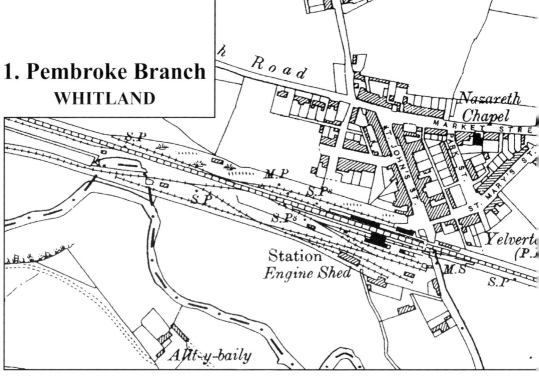

1. Pembroke Branch
WHITLAND

II.　　The 1908 survey at 12ins to 1 mile has the Pembroke branch below the main line and its siding, on the left. There were eight such down sidings by 1950, when a turntable was added to the southern one. The engine shed shown was built by the Pembroke & Tenby Railway, which had its own terminal platform nearby until August 1869. The shed burnt down in 1901 and a replacement was brought from Letterston, in parts. The river was diverted when the branch was built, but the curve in the county boundary remained, as seen.

1.　　A Pembroke branch train is on the left and the roof over it is twice the extent seen, as it continued south to form the goods shed. The other bay platform appears to be signed as GENTLE and in the distance are the signals for Pembroke Junction. The buildings on the right were of GWR origin and were the subject of modernisation by BR. (SLS coll.)

2.   The east end of the up sidings is seen from a down train departing sometime in 1958. A 5500 class 2-6-2T and a 1600 0-6-0PT are preparing a train. The goods sidings lasted until 1972. (D.K.Jones coll.)

3.   The shed which was erected in 1901 had a curved roof and a turntable just outside its door. A new table was provided at the west end of the yard in 1950 and the shed was reroofed. This is the scene on 9th June 1960 with ash being shovelled from under 2-6-2T no. 5520. It has lined green livery and on the left is 0-6-0PT no. 8738. The shed code was sub to 87H (Neyland) and it closed in January 1966. (H.Ballantyne)

4. Major rebuilding took place in 1958 and flat-roofed canopies arrived. Departing for Pembroke on 26th June 1963 is 2-6-2T no. 5571. The coach on the right is on the loop line. The arm with holes was a GWR backing signal. (Bentley coll.)

→ 5. This is East Box, which had 21 levers, and passing it on 28th August 1967 is class 47 no. D1737, with a brake van. The box was replaced by one on the other side of the track on 2nd September 1972. The 43-lever West Box closed the same day and barriers replaced these gates at that time. (R.A.Lumber/D.H.Mitchell)

February 1887

Other views can be found in pictures 23 to 35 in our *Carmarthen to Fishguard* album.

→ 6. Class 101 no. C807 has just arrived from Pembroke Dock on 13th August 1985 and the 1958 structures become apparent. The platform had become a bay in April 1967, when the loop ceased to cross the road. The up bay (right) was not used by passengers after 1962. The branch signals are on the left and the turntable had been in the distance to the left of the main line. (B.I.Nathan)

WHITLAND and CARDIGAN.— Great Western.

Down.

Fares frm Whitland	Down stations	gov mrn	mrn	mrn	turn	aft
1 cl. 2 cl. 3 cl.	CARMRTHN	4 55				
s.d. s.d. s.d.	34 CRMRTHN Jn	5 15				
0 10 0 7 0 5	Whitland dep	6 0	8 10	1 5		6 30
1 6 1 0 0 8	Login	6 18	8 32	1 26		6 48
2 0 1 4 0 11	Llanglydwen	6 27	8 45	1 35		6 57
2 4 1 8 1 1½	Rhydowen	6 32	8 50	1 40	7 2	
2 9 1 11 1 4	Llanfyrnach	6 40	8 59	1 48	7 10	
3 2 2 3 1 6½	Glogue	6 45	9 4	1 53	7 15	
3 7 2 6 1 9	Crymmych A.	6 55	8 45 9 9	12 12 4	7 25	
... ...	Newprt (Ch.)	8 45			9 0	
4 5 3 0 2 2	Boncath	7 9	9 0	12 18	7 39	
5 3 3 8 2 7	Kilgerran	7 20 9 15	12 29	7 50		
5 10 4 1 2 11	Cardigan arr	7 30 9 25	12 40	8 0		

Up.

Up stations	mrn gov	aft	aft
Cardigan dep	7 45 9 40	4 10	
Kilgerran	7 56 9 51	4 21	
Boncath	8 7 10 3	4 33	
Newprt (Ch.)	7 40	2 55	
Crymych Arms	8 20 10 17	3 30 4 47	
Glogue	10 26	3 44 4 56	
Llanfyrnach	8 32 10 31	3 55 5 1	
Rhydowen	10 39	4 10 5 9	
Llanglydwen	8 44 10 44	4 25 5 14	
Login	8 52 10 52	4 40 5 22	
Llanfalteg	9 1 11 1	4 55 5 31	
Whitland 35, 34	9 10 11 10	5 10 5 40	
35 CARMRTHN Ja	10 0 12 13	6 28	
CARMARTHN	10 15 12 30	6 44	

WHITLAND, TENBY, and PEMBROKE.— Pembroke and Tenby.
Sec., Wm. Felix Poole, Carmarthen.   Gen. Man., I. Smedley.   Eng., Lionel R. Wood.

Fares from Whitlnd	Down	gov	mrn	mrn	aft	aft	aft	aft
1 cl. 3 cl.	CRMRTHN T	4 55	8 50	9 50		2 25	5 35	6 30
1 0 0 6½	Narberth	6 14	9 55	10 40	1 22	3 40	6 30	7 37
2 2 1 2	Kilgetty*	6 30	10 10		12 40	3 55	6 45	a
2 6 1 3	Saundrsfoot	6 34	10 15	10 57	12 45	4 0	6 50	7 55
3 4 1 8	Tenby {ar/dp}	6 45 10 30	11 7	12 55	4 15	7 0	5 7	7 0
3 6 1 9	Penally	6 53	a	11 13	1 10	4 0 7	a	8 20
4 2 2 2	Manorbier†	7 2	10 52	11 22	1 22	4 50	7 15	8 35
4 9 2 5	Lamphey	7 10	a	11 30	1 30	4 58	7 22	a
5 0 2 8	Pembroke	7 15	11 5	11 35	1 37	5 3	7 27	8 50
5 0 2 9	Pembrke D.	7 25	11 15	11 45	1 45	5 10	7 35	9 0

a Stop when required for Through Passengers.   Kilgetty and Begelly.

Up	gov	mrn	aft	aft	aft	aft
Pembrke D.	8 5	10 10	12 30	2 30	4 30	6 25
Pembroke	8 13	10 18	12 38	2 40	4 38	6 33
Lamphey	8 17	10 23	a	2 45	4 42	6 37
Manorbier†	8 24	10 29	12 46	2 55	4 50	6 45
Penally	8 32	10 37	12 52	3 5	5 0	6 53
Tenby {ar/dp}	8 35 10 40	12 55 3 10	5 4	6 57		
Saundrafoot	8 49	10 57	1 10	5 16	7 10	
Kilgetty*	8 52	11 0	1 13	a	7 13	
Narbrth [34	8 9	10 11	12 0 1 35	5 857 35		
Whitlnd 35	9 20	11 30	1 50	5 50	7 50	
CRMRTHN Ja	10 0	12 13	2 38	6 28	8 37	
Town	10 15	12 30	2 59	6 44	8 55	

7.　　On the left is a massive dairy complex, which had its own sidings between about 1930 and 1980. The 1972 signal box is largely obscured by the steps on the right, but it was still in use in 2012. We see the single coach of the 17.25 Swansea to Pembroke Dock arriving on 14th June 1994. (T.Heavyside)

8.　　The 1958 up side buildings were recorded on 25th July 2009, although not used for any purpose then. It originally had doors on the other side for access to the booking hall and parcels office. Under the roof is a colour light signal. (V.Mitchell)

NARBERTH

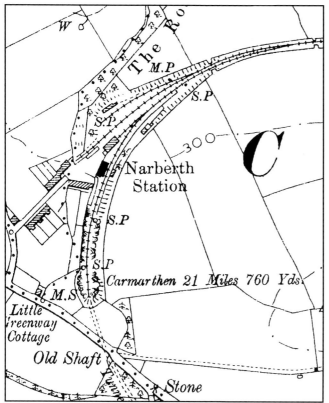

III.　　The 1905 edition at 12ins to 1 mile shows the commencement of the awkward curved tunnel, which is 213yds long and on a gradient of 1 in 52 to Cold Blow Summit. The population was steady at just over 1000 for the first half of the twentieth century.

9.　　The up building and goods shed as seen were completed in July 1878. The fire buckets are hung traditionally on the outside of the gents, where water was always on tap. The staff numbered six for most of the 1930s.
(Lens of Sutton coll.)

10.   There were two docks; the siding to this one leads off the down loop and is seen in about 1958. Passengers for Tenby and beyond had to use the crossing in the foreground. (R.S.Carpenter coll.)

11.   The photographer was on a train from Whitland on 26th September 1961, while a goods train bound for there waits at the up platform. We gain a closer look at the down dock and the permanent way hut. This siding lasted until 19th December 1963. (Bentley coll.)

12. Part of the village is evident, as we examine the small signal box, which contained just 13 levers. It was in use until 3rd October 1965 and is seen in about 1960. (R.S.Carpenter coll.)

Narberth	1903	1913	1923	1933
Passenger tickets issued	22684	20234	19580	10650
Season tickets issued	*	*	27	35
Parcels forwarded	11551	19151	39633	35166
General goods forwarded (tons)	862	681	780	436
Coal and coke received (tons)	2733	2467	1094	1598
Other minerals received (tons)	1086	1050	1320	2568
General goods received (tons)	4476	4404	5267	6170
Coal and Coke handled	196	470	1368	932
Trucks of livestock handled	529	597	343	182

December 1947

13.   Staffing ceased on 28th September 1964 and the goods yard closed on 7th June 1965. Its site was in the background and this was later used by a farm machinery business. No. W51099 is working the 14.55 Whitland to Pembroke Dock on 27th June 1981. (T.Heavyside)

14.   The down platform had been taken out of use in October 1965 and the up one is seen on 25th July 2009. The main building was in residential use and the remaining platform would accommodate four coaches. (V.Mitchell)

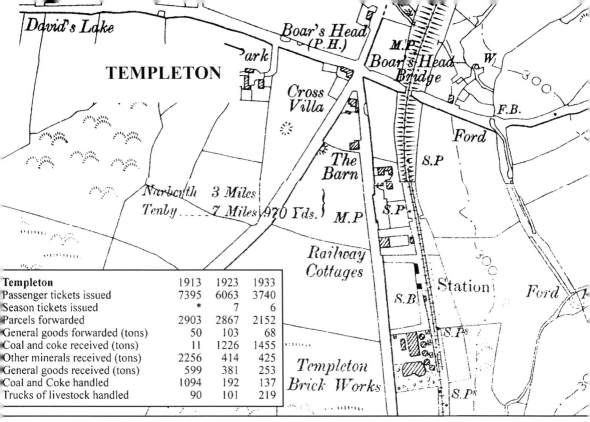

Templeton

Templeton	1913	1923	1933
Passenger tickets issued	7395	6063	3740
Season tickets issued	*	7	6
Parcels forwarded	2903	2867	2152
General goods forwarded (tons)	50	103	68
Coal and coke received (tons)	11	1226	1455
Other minerals received (tons)	2256	414	425
General goods received (tons)	599	381	253
Coal and Coke handled	1094	192	137
Trucks of livestock handled	90	101	219

IV. Trains stopped here from the opening, but usually only on market days. The building was completed in 1867 and trains appeared in the timetable in October 1877. Bradshaw showed a service on Fridays and Saturdays until 30th April 1906. This 1908 extract is at 12 ins to 1 mile and includes a site producing silica firebricks. It closed in 1924 and its rail traffic ceased.

15. The suffix PLATFORM was used until 1905, when the signal box came into use. The saddle tank is standing on the reversible goods loop, alongside which is a short siding. There were two men here in the 1930s. (Lens of Sutton coll.)

16.   The down platform was opened on 1st February 1915, the siding having been moved further east and lengthened. The signal box had 29 levers and was photographed on 22nd May 1963. (P.J.Garland/R.S.Carpenter)

17.   A view south from the same period has a very long down siding in the distance; this was of value during periods of heavy military traffic. The goods service was withdrawn on 2nd December 1963, passenger trains ceased to call after 15th June 1964 and the signal box closed on 3rd October 1965, when the down loop was taken out of use. (Lens of Sutton coll.)

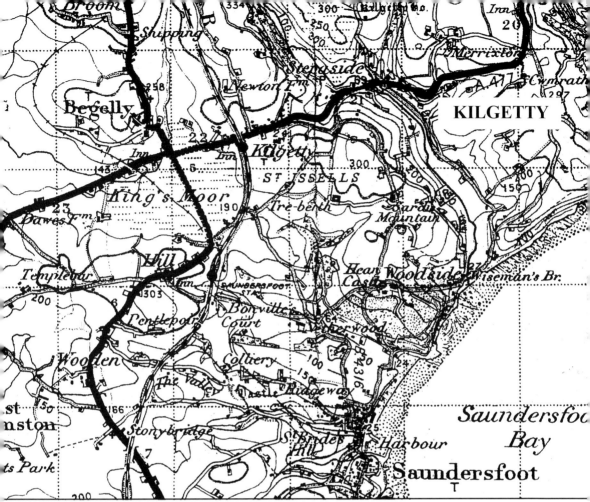

V.   The station is close to the bridge over the A477 on this 1946 edition at 2ins to 1 mile. Saundersfoot station is only ½ mile south of it. In the top left part of the map is a length of the Saundersfoot Railway, but the remainder is less clear. Earlier it had a line along the coast to Woodside and then inland to Stepaside.

18.   The well ventilated station was on the down side of the line, but the original platform was on the up side. There had been a signal box on the platform seen until 1895 and there was a single siding behind the camera until June 1965. The layout included a loop and a cattle pen.
(Lens of Sutton coll.)

19.   The 10.55am from Paddington arrives on 8th July 1958, carrying the "Pembroke Coast Express" headboard. This name was introduced in 1953 and staffing ceased here on 28th September 1964. (R.M.Casserley)

→ 20. No. 158828 calls with the 09.50 Swansea to Pembroke Dock. A painter is attending to the rusty GWR spear fencing on 24th July 2008. There were four employees in the 1930s. (A.C.Hartless)

→   21. A small crowd prepares to join the 14.55 from Pembroke Dock to Paddington HST on 25th July 2009. The suffix "& Belgelley" was used until 1901. (V.Mitchell)

Kilgetty	1903	1913	1923	1933
Passenger tickets issued	14169	15715	17443	7783
Season tickets issued	*	*	83	37
Parcels forwarded	2181	2859	9192	8927
General goods forwarded (tons)	206	121	547	224
Coal and coke received (tons)	4973	759	261	722
Other minerals received (tons)	623	680	1203	1591
General goods received (tons)	1889	2270	2639	2137
Coal and Coke handled	502	434	487	644
Trucks of livestock handled	19	121	228	98

3rd SINGLE   **SINGLE 3rd**

KILGETTY to

KILGETTY   KILGETTY

Saundersfoot   Saunderafoot

SAUNDERSFOOT

(W)   2d.   FARE   2d. (W)

For Conditions see over For Conditions see over

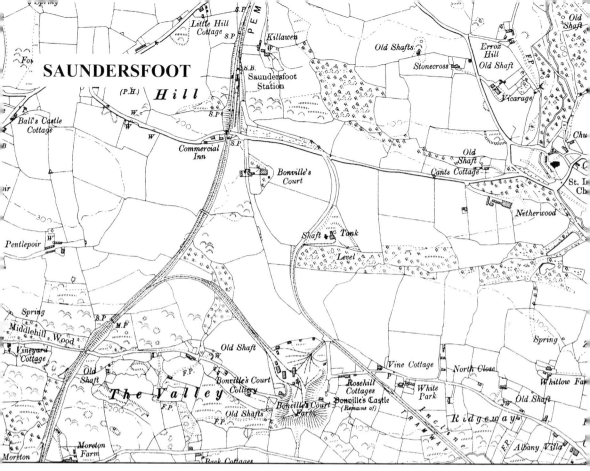

VI. The 1908 survey at 6ins to 1 mile has our route from top to bottom, with a branch to Bonville's Court Colliery. To the right of this is part of the Saundersfoot Railway, but marked as a tramway. Several shafts are also shown. The station had been near the lower left corner of the map until 1868.

Saundersfoot	1903	1913	1923	1933
Passenger tickets issued	15236	16342	16610	4999
Season tickets issued	*	*	45	8
Parcels forwarded	2942	4236	5010	5677
General goods forwarded (tons)	158	107	163	152
Coal and coke received (tons)	103	190	287	284
Other minerals received (tons)	44	111	350	733
General goods received (tons)	761	1460	1221	753
Coal and Coke handled	900	230	1613	315
Trucks of livestock handled	4	1	-	-

22. Extensive Army camps were a feature of the district for many generations and much railway revenue was generated from them, also from the Navy at Pembroke. Uniforms prevail in this postcard view of the down platform. Four men had GWR ones in the 1930s. (Lens of Sutton coll.)

23.	Bonville's Court Colliery was the largest in the Pembrokeshire coalfield and is seen in 1907. The county's output in tons was: 1875-80,000; 1885-100,000; 1900-50,000; 1930-30,000 and 1948-500. This pit opened in 1842 and closed on 17th April 1930. Naked flames were used here for lighting, but only one minor explosion was noted. The area produced high quality anthracite. (British Railways)

24.	Departing south on 13th June 1959 is 4300 class 2-6-0 no. 7320. The Saundersfoot Railway had a tunnel under the main line in this vicinity. The station was unstaffed from 28th September 1964. (D.K.Jones coll.)

25.   We are on the up platform on 20th June 1962 and have the 12-lever signal box on the left. There were three short sidings behind the down platform until closure of the yard on 2nd December 1963. The rodding tunnel is unusually arched. (R.G.Nelson/T.Walsh)

26.   A view in the other direction on the same day includes the parcels shed and van. All buildings have long gone and a standard shelter provided on the down platform. The up line and the box were taken out of use on 3rd October 1965. (R.G.Nelson/T.Walsh)

SAUNDERSFOOT RAILWAY

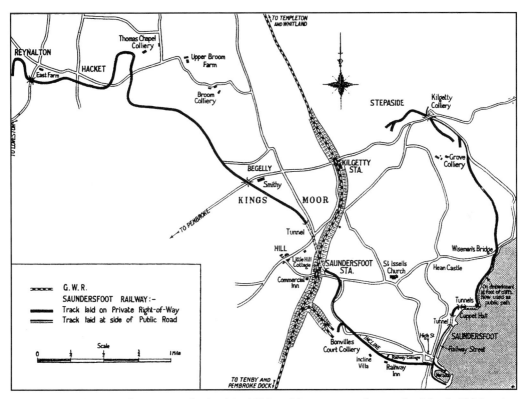

VII.   The 4ft gauge line was authorised in 1829 and began operating on 1st March 1834, using horses. It carried the anthracite for loading on to ships in the harbour. Much of this was destined for breweries in Southeast England and tin makers in Cornwall. Reynalton Colliery was open from 1914 to 1921. Moreton Colliery sidings had been near the bottom of the map until 1887.

27.   Railway Street ran parallel to the coast and carried the line from Stepaside. The driver of the 1874 Manning Wardle 0-4-0ST devoted to that line appears to be glaring at a car parked too far from the kerb. Another engine was bought in 1914, from Kerr Stuart, for the higher section of track. (Railway Magazine)

28.   The cable-worked incline is marked on the maps and was graded at 1 in 5. The railway also carried miners and iron ore. The three rails became four halfway up the incline, for a short distance, to enable wagons to pass. (Railway Magazine)

29.   The 1874 locomotive was recorded on the sea front in the mid-1930s. Some of the ancient drams behind it had grooves worn into their wheels, often very deeply. (M.J.Stretton coll.)

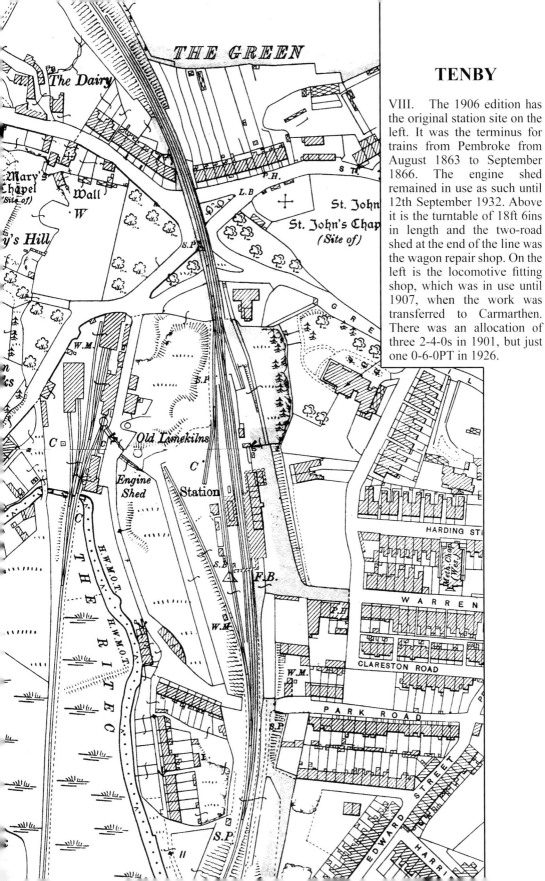

TENBY

VIII. The 1906 edition has the original station site on the left. It was the terminus for trains from Pembroke from August 1863 to September 1866. The engine shed remained in use as such until 12th September 1932. Above it is the turntable of 18ft 6ins in length and the two-road shed at the end of the line was the wagon repair shop. On the left is the locomotive fitting shop, which was in use until 1907, when the work was transferred to Carmarthen. There was an allocation of three 2-4-0s in 1901, but just one 0-6-0PT in 1926.

30.   This view north is from the footbridge and is probably from the Edwardian era. The population of the town was a little over 4500 in the Aprils of both 1901 and 1961, but rose greatly in the Summer months. The rear coach is a LNWR one bound for Manchester. (Lens of Sutton coll.)

31.   A panorama in the other direction in the same era includes some intricate tracery in the canopy brackets. On the right is the 25-lever signal box, which was open until 25th March 1956. The staff numbered 14 for most of the 1930s. (Lens of Sutton coll.)

32.   Running in with freight from Pembroke Dock in about 1960 is 2-6-2T no. 5549. Above its cab is the junction with the original route, this passing through the bushes on the right. Black Rock is in the right background and a quarry thereon had a siding until its closure in the mid-1920s. The route is obscured by caravans. (R.S.Carpenter)

33.   A northward record from May 1963 includes a Royal Mail Morris van awaiting the arrival of a down train. There was a short dock at the far end of that platform, once used by the gentry for the horse and carriage. (P.J.Garland/R.S.Carpenter)

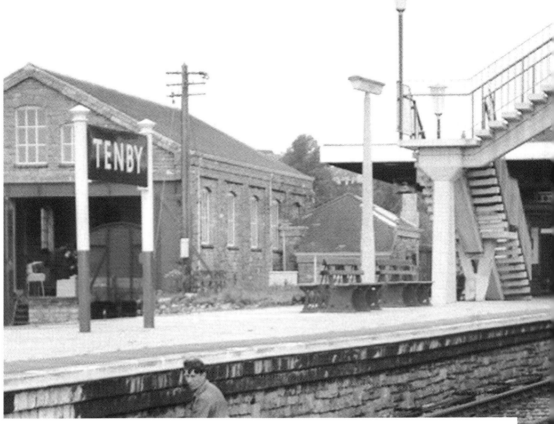

34. In addition to 4-6-0 no. 7804 *Baydon Manor*, items of interest include the new up buildings, concrete footbridge and canopy from 1959 and the "Upper Yard" goods shed and yard, which remained in use until 7th November 1966. There was a 3-ton crane there. (Lens of Sutton coll.)

35. The date is 20th August 1972 and no. 1555 is working the 17.55 return excursion to Plymouth. The dock siding is in the grass and further left are two camping coaches, on an isolated section of track. (R.A.Lumber/D.H.Mitchell coll.)

THE PEMBROKE COAST EXPRESS

RESTAURANT CAR SERVICE (¶)

LONDON, NEWPORT, CARDIFF, SWANSEA, TENBY and PEMBROKE DOCK

WEEK DAYS

		E	S			
		am	am			pm
LONDON (Paddington)	dep	10A55	10A55	Pembroke Dock .. .. ..dep		1A 5
		pm	pm	Pembroke.. .. .. „		1A10
Newport	arr	1 6	1 47	Lamphey .. .. „		1 15
Cardiff (General) ..	..„	1 25	2 8	Manorbier .. .. „		1A25
Swansea (High St.) ..	..„	2 40	3 28	Penally .. .. „		1A32
Llanelly	..„	3 12	4 5	Tenby .. .. „		1A40
Carmarthen	..„	3 40	4 34	Saundersfoot .. .. „		1A50
St. Clears	..„	4 0	4 52	Kilgetty .. .. „		1A55
Whitland	..„	4 10	5 2	Templeton .. .. „		2 0
Narberth	..„	4 27	5 20	Narberth .. .. „		2A10
Templeton	..„	4 37	5 30	Whitland .. .. „		2A25
Kilgetty	..„	4 43	5 36	Carmarthen .. .. „		2 48
Saundersfoot	..„	4 45	5 39	Llanelly .. .. „		3 15
Tenby	..„	4 55	5 47	Swansea (High Street) .. .. „		3A45
Penally	..„	5 1	5 54	Cardiff (General) .. .. .. „		5 0
Manorbier	..„	5 9	6 2	Newport .. .. „		5 20
Lamphey	..„	5 15	6 8	LONDON (Paddington) .. arr		7B45
Pembroke..	..„	5 18	6 13			
Pembroke Dock ..	..„	5 26	6 19			

A—Seats can be reserved in advance on payment of a fee of 2s. 0d. per seat (see page 27).
B—On Saturdays calls at Slough 7.39, Ealing (Broadway), 7.59 and arrives Paddington 8.13 p.m.
E—Except Saturdays.
S—Saturdays only.
¶—Restaurant Car available between London (Paddington) and Swansea (High St.), in each direction.

36.　　After arriving with the 08.24 from York on 27th June 1981, no. 47147 is shunting the stock to form the 18.20 to Swansea. The box had 25 levers and was in use until 10th December 1988. The train is on the bridge over Park Road. The up loop (right) had lost its southern connection to the main line in May 1968. (T.Heavyside)

37.　　No. 47254 is leaving with empty stock for Swansea on the same day and is seen on Tenby Viaduct. This has seven arches and is 136yds long. (T.Heavyside)

38.   The goods shed (left) and the yard become premises of a builders merchant. The concrete footbridge had arrived in 1960, replacing the one of 1896, which was built of steel. This shows the transition in DMU types in the early 1980s. Left is no. C616 and right is no. C814. (N.W.Sprinks)

39.   The main building from 1866 was of P&TR design, but the canopies were GWR additions. The photograph is from 3rd September 2001 and has the passenger entrance near the ticket machine. (C.L.Caddy)

40.		The down platform was photographed from an HST in July 2009, the notable feature being the windowless cabin housing the single line equipment, which was self-service for drivers, for a token release. The concrete footbridge had been replaced by a welded steel structure. (V.Mitchell)

Tenby	1903	1913	1923	1933
Passenger tickets issued	71129	63430	63002	37135
Season tickets issued	*	*	170	102
Parcels forwarded	25733	41758	39409	46013
General goods forwarded (tons)	931	994	720	991
Coal and coke received (tons)	4833	2004	4621	1699
Other minerals received (tons)	530	644	1226	1807
General goods received (tons)	3732	4787	4391	3500
Coal and Coke handled	1122	2870	2004	6172
Trucks of livestock handled	2708	3582	3021	2738

Traff. Man., I. Smedley.]		PEMBROKE and TENBY.		[Sec., T. Stokes.

Up. Week Days.

Up.	mrn	mrn	aft	aft	aft	S n aft
Pembroke Dock d	8 5	1030	4 15	6 15	0 3	5 15
Pembroke	8 13	1038	4 23	6 23	8	5 23
Lamphey [Flrence	8 17	1042	4 27	6 27	8 17	5 27
Manorbier, for St.	8 26	1052	4 36	6 36	8 21	5 37
Penally	8 34	11 1	4 45	6 45	8 30	5 46
Tenby ...... { arr	8 38	11 5	4 49	6 50	8 35	5 50
{ dep	8 42	1110	4 52	6 55	....	5 3
Saundersfoot	8 50	1121	5 1	7 5	....	5 10
Kilgetty & Begelly	8 53	1124	a	7 8	....	5 12
Templeton	....	....	F.S.	....	....	....
Narberth	9 9	1142	5 21	7 25	....	5 33
Whitland 28, { a	9 21	1154	5 31	7 35	....	5 45
29 { d	9 25	1159	....	7 37	....	....
St. Clears	9 37	1241	....	7 49	....	....
Carmarthen 130 a	9 55	1225	....	8 7	....	....

Down.	mrn	mrn	c	c	aft	S n aft
Carmarthen..dep	....	8 55	1230	5 30	....	..
St. Clears	....	9 10	1245	5 45	....	..
Whitland .. { arr	....	9 20	1255	5 55	....	..
{ dep	6 15	9 45	1 0	6 5	....	7 15
Narberth	6 30	10 0	1 15	6 19	....	7 30
Templeton	F.S.	Sat.	....	....	....	....
Kilgetty & Begelly	6 46	1016	1 31	b	....	7 46
Saundersfoot	6 49	1020	1 34	6 36	....	7 50
Tenby .... { arr	7 0	1030	1 43	6 45	....	7 58
{ dep	7 20	1035	1 45	6 50	8 45	8 0
Penally [Florence	7 28	1038	1 43	6 53	8 48	8 3
Manorbier, for St.	7 32	1052	1 57	7 0	8 57	8 12
Lamphey	7 40	11 0	2 5	7 9	5 8	8 22
Pembroke	7 45	11 5	2 10	7 10	9 8	8 25
Pembroke Dock a	7 53	1115	2 20	7 20	9 18	8 35

c 3rd-class to St. Clears and Whitland.

a Stops by signal to take up thro' Pass.		b Sets down thro' Pass. on informing Guard at Whitlan

August 1871

SOUTH OF TENBY

41.   The branch was the original route to the terminus and the ground frame was called Black Rock Sidings. The siding trailed from the branch to reach the quarry, which was beyond the left border. (P.J.Garland/R.S.Carpenter)

WHITLAND, TENBY, and PEMBROKE.—Pembroke and Tenby.
Wm. Felix Poole. Gen. Man.,   Eng. & Loco. Supt., Lionel R. Wood.

Down.		Week Days.					Sn		Up.		Week Days.					Sn
	gov	mrn	aft	aft	aft	aft	gov			gov	mrn	aft	aft	aft	aft	aft
CARMARTHEN T.	4 45	9 5	1 0	2 30	4 30	6 20	aft		Pembroke Dock.	8 0	1045	1230	2 30	4 30	6 0	8 0
„ JUNC. 56	5 1	9 19	1 8	2 47	4 39	6 34	....	2	Pembroke	8 6	1051	1238	2 40	4 37	6 6	8 8
Whitland ..dep.	5 45	10 0	1 40	3 25	5 15	7 30	7 30	3½	Lamphey	8 10	1055	1242	2 44	4 41	6 10	8 12
Narberth	5 55	1010	1 50	3 40	5 30	7 40	7 40	7	Manorbier	8 17	11 2	1250	2 52	4 49	6 18	8 21
Kilgetty*	6 10	1025	2 2	3 52	5 42	7 52	7 52	10½	Penally	8 25	1110	1258	3 0	4 57	6 26	8 30
Saundersfoot....	6 15	1030	2 5	3 56	5 47	7 57	7 55	11½	Tenby.... {arr.	8 23	1113	1 2	3 5	5 0	6 30	8 35
Tenby.... {arr. dep.	6 25	1040	2 15	4 6	5 57	8 7	8 5		{dep.	8 35	1120	1 10	3 10	5 5	6 35	8 30
Penally	6 33	1053	2 21	4 14	6 5	8 15	8 20	15½	Saundersfoot....	8 44	1 3	1 7	....	5 14	6 46	6 40
Manorbier	6 40	11 2	2 29	4 22	6 17	8 25	8 35	16½	Kilgetty*	8 47	1133	2 ..	..	5 17	6 ..	44
Lamphey	6 47	11 5	2 36	4 30	6 24	8 32	8 43	22	Narberth	9 0	1143	1 ..	..	5 33	7 2	6 59
Pembroke	6 52	1118	2 42	4 40	6 28	8 37	8 50	27¼	Whitland 55, 56	9 10	1153	2 0	3 55	5 45	7 12	7 10
Pembroke Dock.	7 0	1120	2 50	4 50	6 35	8 45	9 0	41	55 CARMARTHEN Jn.	9 49	1234	2 41	4 42	6 30	8 0	8 0
								42	„ Town	1010	1250	3 0	4 55	6 44	8 15	....

Kilgetty and Begelly

42.   Black Rock Quarry produced limestone, which was far from black. Additional sidings were added on the left in 1899 to serve limekilns, but traffic ceased in the 1920s. (British Railways)

43.   The end of the branch is seen in May 1936, the terminal building having become a wagon repair shop. Known as "Lower Yard", the area was used for goods traffic until 7th June 1965 and eventually became a car park. Until the coming of the P&TR, the town could be reached twice a month by ferry from Bristol. (W.A.Camwell)

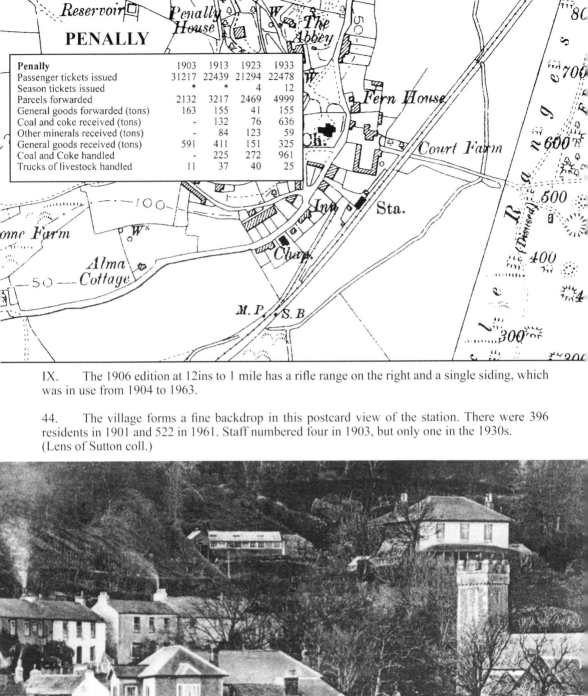

The Glen

Reservoir

PENALLY

Penally House

The Abbey

Fern House

Court Farm

Range

80
700
600
500
400
300

50

Inn
Sta.
Ch.

one Farm

Alma Cottage

50

Chap.

M.P. S.B

Penally	1903	1913	1923	1933
Passenger tickets issued	31217	22439	21294	22478
Season tickets issued	*	*	4	12
Parcels forwarded	2132	3217	2469	4999
General goods forwarded (tons)	163	155	41	155
Coal and coke received (tons)	-	132	76	636
Other minerals received (tons)	-	84	123	59
General goods received (tons)	591	411	151	325
Coal and Coke handled	-	225	272	961
Trucks of livestock handled	11	37	40	25

IX.   The 1906 edition at 12ins to 1 mile has a rifle range on the right and a single siding, which was in use from 1904 to 1963.

44.   The village forms a fine backdrop in this postcard view of the station. There were 396 residents in 1901 and 522 in 1961. Staff numbered four in 1903, but only one in the 1930s. (Lens of Sutton coll.)

45.   Here and at Tenby, the platforms could take seven coaches. There were camping coaches in the siding during most Summers until 1964, war years excepted. This record is from about 1960. (Lens of Sutton coll.)

46.   The main building was sold as a house and is seen on 14th June 1994 in the company of the 11.16 from Swansea. The station was first in Bradshaw in October 1863, closed from 16th June 1964 to 29th June 1970, from 16th November 1970 to 5th April 1971 and from 13th September 1971 to 28th February 1972, but has remained open since. (T.Heavyside)

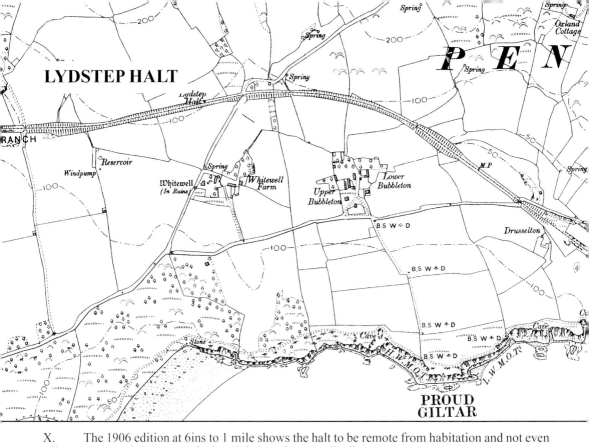

LYDSTEP HALT

X.　　The 1906 edition at 6ins to 1 mile shows the halt to be remote from habitation and not even adjacent to a road. However, the beach is less than ½ mile distant.

47.　　The halt was available for excursions and picnics from 1873 and was open for regular use from 1st May 1905. It was closed in the Winters from September 1908 and fully from September 1914. It was open again from July 1923 until January 1956 and is seen in January 1961. (Stations UK)

MANORBIER

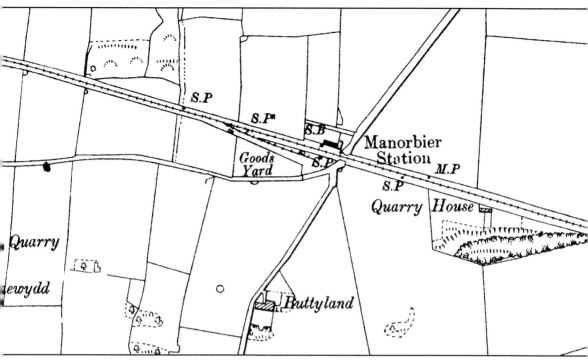

XI.   The 1906 survey indicates one siding and no loop. Another siding and a loop came soon. There were five employees here in the 1930s.

48.   Two photographs from 20th June 1962 show the facilities at their optimum. This includes the signal box, which had a 12-lever frame, and was in use until 3rd October 1965. Beyond it is the lamp room. (R.G.Nelson/T.Walsh)

49.   Now we look east and can see a camping coach. The last one here was in the Summer of 1964. There had been four-wheelers here in 1937-39, when the GWR used the term "camp coach", not camping. (R.G.Nelson/T.Walsh)

50.   Staffing ceased on 28th September 1964 and the loop and the sidings were taken out of use in October 1965. This is the sad scene on 24th August 1967, when train crews had to open the gates themselves. (C.L.Caddy)

51.　　Automatic Open Crossing Remotely Monitored is the term used for the arrangements seen in 2009. The buildings were well restored and used as a dwelling. The platform was fit for five coaches. (V.Mitchell)

Manorbier	1903	1913	1923	1933
Passenger tickets issued	17637	13918	16195	7300
Season tickets issued	*	*	98	13
Parcels forwarded	2239	2483	1754	2261
General goods forwarded (tons)	22	134	73	36
Coal and coke received (tons)	710	505	471	835
Other minerals received (tons)	177	123	148	343
General goods received (tons)	277	503	288	320
Coal and Coke handled	101	12	270	511
Trucks of livestock handled	4	18	19	4

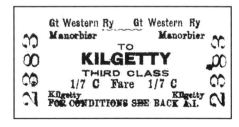

BEAVERS HILL HALT

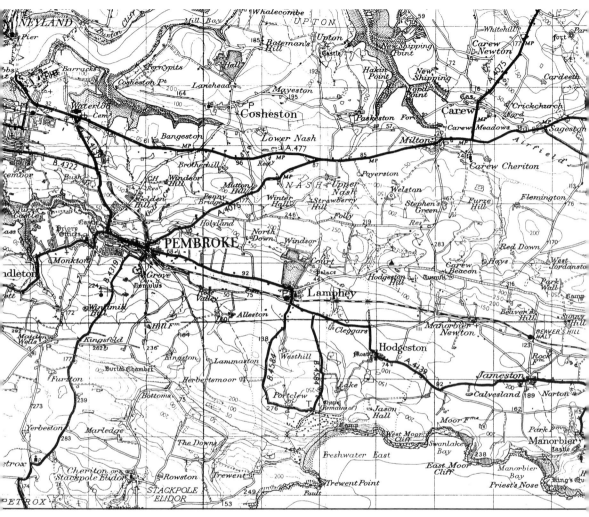

XII.   The 1952 edition at 1ins to 1 mile emphasises the low level of population around three stops. Manorbier Castle has for long been popular with visitors, but is remote from its station.

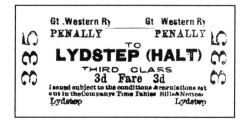

52.   The halt was open from 1st May 1905 to 21st September 1914 and again from 1st December 1923 until 15th June 1964. It is seen in poor condition in 1961. The 1947 timetable offered a down train at 12.2pm (Fridays only) and an up one at 4.14pm, weekdays only.

53.   The level crossing was "open" from June 1965 and has remained so. There are six similar crossings in two miles, although now devoid of ropes. (Lens of Sutton coll.)

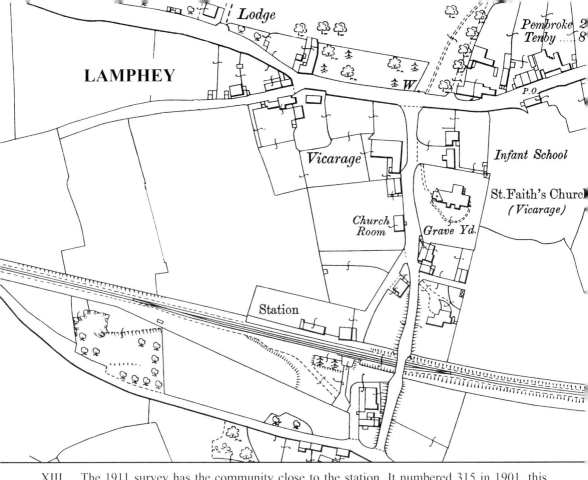

XIII.   The 1911 survey has the community close to the station. It numbered 315 in 1901, this rising to 418 by 1961. One can see a road alignment that predates the bridge.

54.   Steam railmotors of this type operated on the branch from 1905 to 1914; this one has a small coach trailing, so it will have to run round at both ends of its journey. (Lens of Sutton coll.)

55.   There were usually two men here in 1903-35, but one only in 1936-38. Records show a signal box between the buildings until about 1897, but there is no rodding tunnel. The cattle pen arrived in 1906. (Lens of Sutton coll.)

56.   We finish the visit with two pictures from 20th June 1962. There were camping coaches here most Summers until 1964; it seems that they had not yet arrived for the season. Goods traffic continued to use the loop on the left until 2nd December 1963, but was light. (RG.Nelson/T.Walsh)

Lamphey	1903	1913	1923	1933
Passenger tickets issued	526	485	1041	1097
Season tickets issued	15224	13440	14137	7758
Parcels forwarded	719	676	772	2587
General goods forwarded (tons)	27	18	14	14
Coal and coke received (tons)	251	154	119	272
Other minerals received (tons)	13	77	112	431
General goods received (tons)	109	101	95	61
Coal and Coke handled	34	30	43	130
Trucks of livestock handled	7	36	42	11

Pembroke	1903	1913	1923	193
Passenger tickets issued	12176	12688	22443	184
Season tickets issued	90901	163117	128837	1846
Parcels forwarded	15892	23123	21245	2459
General goods forwarded (tons)	944	1048	1712	5
Coal and coke received (tons)	6237	5193	3876	336
Other minerals received (tons)	783	665	1575	273
General goods received (tons)	3086	3717	5595	774
Coal and Coke handled	1119	1534	3839	328
Trucks of livestock handled	263	418	570	4

57.   Staffing ceased on 28th September 1964 and the station was converted to a house. A platform for five coaches was retained and a standard hut provided. (R.G.Nelson/T.Walsh)

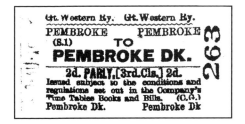

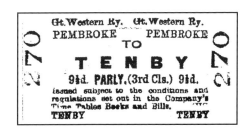

PEMBROKE

XIV.   Scaled at 12ins to 1 mile, the 1948 edition
includes the centre of the historic town and shows
the importance of water and stone to its earlier
life. The number of residents fell from 15,853 in
1901 to 13,500 in 1961, presumably largely due to
reduction in military presence.

Extract from *Bradshaw's Guide of 1866*.
(Reprinted by Middleton Press.)

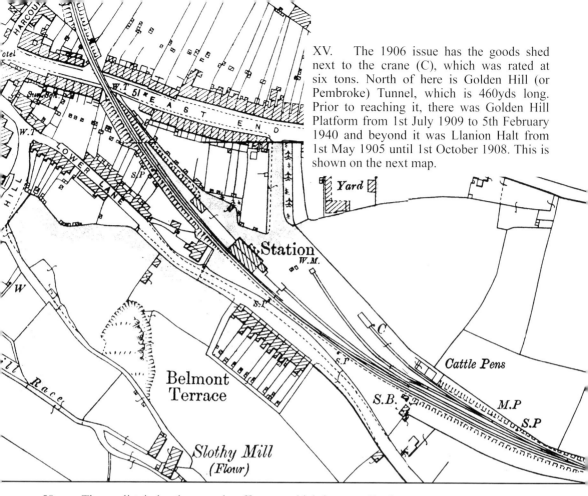

XV.   The 1906 issue has the goods shed next to the crane (C), which was rated at six tons. North of here is Golden Hill (or Pembroke) Tunnel, which is 460yds long. Prior to reaching it, there was Golden Hill Platform from 1st July 1909 to 5th February 1940 and beyond it was Llanion Halt from 1st May 1905 until 1st October 1908. This is shown on the next map.

58.   The cyclist is by the parcels office on which hangs a Rochester pattern gas globe. Fine stonework and a cantilevered canopy could be enjoyed on 20th June 1962. There had been 9 or 10 men here in the 1930s. (R.G.Nelson/T.Walsh)

59.   The goods shed was made of iron and erected in 1890. The signal box was in use from 1895 until 5th September 1971, when it had 16 levers. The goods yard closed on 1st January 1969 and became a car park. (R.G.Nelson/T.Walsh coll.)

60.   The 09.05 from Swansea was recorded on 14th June 1994, along with a grander shelter than elsewhere and tasteful replica Suggs gas lamp housings. (T.Heavyside)

PEMBROKE DOCK

XVI. The 1909 edition at 12ins to 1 mile has the station and the gasworks across the join of the pages. The 55ft 1902 turntable is close to "West Lanion" and the engine shed is near to the junction of Hobbs Point branch, but is not annotated. The Naval Dockyard is shown as the white space on the left, for security reasons.

Hobbs Point

Mud

B.S⁺ A ⋏ D

Pier

West Lanion Fill

Mud

Mud

Mud

Mud

Martello Tower
(Disused)

FRONT STREET

DOCK

COMMERCIAL ROW

KING STREET

QUEEN STREET

QUEEN STREET

DIMOND STREET

CLARENCE STREET

WELLINGTON STREET

BREWERY STREET

PARK STREET

MEYRICK STREET

LEWIS STREET

WATER STREET

GWYTHER STREET

KIN

Chap.

ALBION SQ.

Sch.

CHARLTON PLACE

BUSH STREET

CHURCH STREET

LAWS STREET

STREET

MARKET STREET

PEMBROKE STREET

Reservoirs

CEMETERY
(Disused)

Ch.

Sch.

Chap.

DOCK

B.S. B ⋏ O

61. Familiar barge boards and other architectural details can be enjoyed again, along with some rare gas lanterns in the entrance. Pity about the excessive ivy, though. (Lens of Sutton coll.)

62. This panorama may be from around 1903, when there was a staff of 22. In the 1930s, it dropped from 17 to 15. Sadly, no details are available, but the view is from the 1902 33-lever signal box. (Lens of Sutton coll.)

Pembroke Dock	1903	1913	1923	1933
Passenger tickets issued	95067	110377	115728	38726
Season tickets issued	*	*	187	14
Parcels forwarded	27929	42337	40739	41953
General goods forwarded (tons)	3047	5496	3703	1943
Coal and coke received (tons)	12172	8857	5137	909
Other minerals received (tons)	4738	3709	1797	2405
General goods received (tons)	16830	17709	8608	6830
Coal and Coke handled	7200	6299	7109	10613
Trucks of livestock handled	2	-	5	3

63.   The crew of a railmotor pose, sometime between 1905 and 1914, while the six-ton crane was at rest. The gas lamp had been changed since the previous view. The gasworks dated from 1851 and had a siding by 1903, when the coal delivered was 5500 tons per annum. The demand had risen to 6678 tons by 1947. The works was replaced by a grid supply in 1957. (NRM)

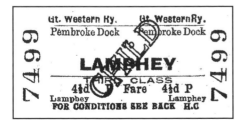

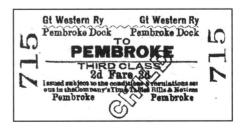

64.   No. 5520 stands with the 3.50pm to Whitland on 8th June 1960, by which time electric lighting had arrived. The line to the dockyard continues beyond the end of the train. The Admiralty opened the depot in 1830 and it was employing 3000 men by the 1860s. (H.Ballantyne)

→ 65. Taken minutes later from the same train, this view includes the connection to Hobbs Point. There was a siding on that line to an Army ordnance depot for many years. Over the pit is 2-6-2T no. 4107. The shed was coded sub to 87H and closed on 9th September 1963. The three sidings in the distance were for carriages. (H.Ballantyne)

→   66. The coal stage was recorded in May 1963, along with a coaling crane. The allocation in 1947 was two 2-6-2Ts. The shed received a timber extension at the rear in 1902. (P.J.Garland/R.S.Carpenter)

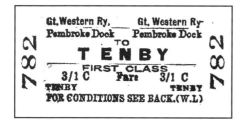

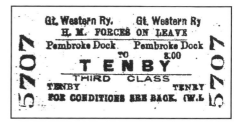

67.　　The toilet cistern of an express coach is being filled on 21st May 1963, while other hoses lie on the platform. The gap between the buildings in the distance is the location of the first level crossing on the line to the Dockyard. It carried traffic from 1871 and became Admiralty property in 1892, closing in 1970. (P.J.Garland/R.S.Carpenter)

68.　　Moving to the west end of the platform on the same day, we see the gates of the crossing over Water Street. The crossing in the foreground is between the two platforms and was seldom used by passengers. The weighbridge was to the right of the lorry. (P.J.Garland/R.S.Carpenter)

69.   Looking in the other direction on 26th June 1963, we see the rough crossing more fully, along with 4-6-0 no. 7826 *Longworth Manor*. The RAF had been active in the area since 1930, notably with flying boats. An exhibition centre for these monsters has recently been established locally. (N.K.Harrop/Bentley coll.)

70.   A local train was recorded on 5th August 1972, along with the disused goods shed, which would soon be demolished. There had earlier been much anti-aircraft and anti-submarine training undertaken in the area. All freight on the branch ceased in 1978. (E.Wilmshurst)

71.   The canopy was a GWR addition in 1902 and is seen on 13th August 1980, following the arrival of the 08.50 from Whitland. In the distance had been the 33-lever signal box, which functioned as such until 24th August 1966. (D.H.Mitchell)

➜   72. Many of the same features of Tenby station can be seen in this fine view from 26th June 1981. No. 37222 is arriving with the 16.10 from Swansea and it will soon use the line on the left to run round its train. (T.Heavyside)

➜   73. We move forward to 14th June 1994, when few locomotives were to be seen. No. 153380 forms the 11.16 to Swansea, while Pembroke Castle continues to be an important visitor attraction. (T.Heavyside)

74.   It is 25th July 2009 and no. 43180 is silent after arriving with the 08.45 from Paddington at 14.14. It will leave at 14.55, offering one of the finest day trips from the capitals of both England and Wales. There was a crossover under the middle of the train, used mainly by the engineers. (V.Mitchell)

75.   Seen on the same day, the terminus had been renovated in 1979, when the B&I ferry service to Cork was introduced. It started on 22nd May and a bus connection was provided initially. (V.Mitchell)

Cardigan Branch
WEST OF WHITLAND

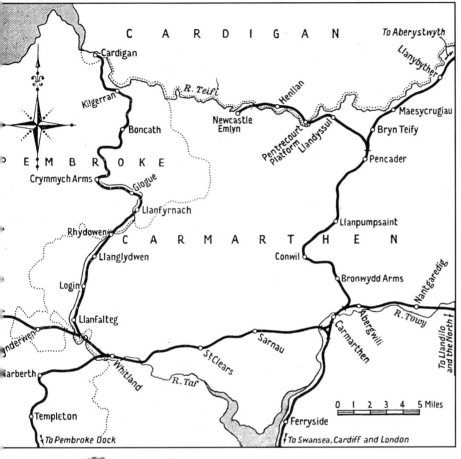

XVII. The 1952 map shows that only the final half mile of the branch was in Cardiganshire.

76. A view west on 25th May 1963 has the branch curving right from the main line. The curved bar from the white post was termed the "cow horn" and was used to catch the single line staff pouch hoop, when held out by a passing engineman. The box closed on 28th July 1964. (P.J.Garland/ R.S.Carpenter)

LLANFALTEG

Spring
Llwyn-celyn

Rhyd-yr-Esgob
P.O.
Inn
F.B.
Spring
Bwlch-melyn
Station
S.P^s
Llanfalteg
d-tir-du

Llanfalteg	1903	1913	1923	1
Passenger tickets issued	5906	5516	5495	3
Season tickets issued	*	*	24	
Parcels forwarded	1319	9520	15970	14
General goods forwarded (tons)	509	100	170	
Coal and coke received (tons)	480	573	433	
Other minerals received (tons)	179	254	988	
General goods received (tons)	365	345	658	
Coal and Coke handle	38	65	82	
Trucks of livestock handled	1	-	1	

XVIII. We enter the area of Welsh place names on the 1907 edition at 12ins to 1 mile. It includes a small engine shed (close to S.Ps), but this had closed in 1897.

77. The single siding appears in both these views from about 1962. Well overgrown, it was officially in use until the end of passenger services on 10th April 1962. (Lens of Sutton coll.)

78. There had been a 13-lever signal box here earlier, but this ground frame had sufficed for many years. Four men were employed here in the 1930s.
(Lens of Sutton coll.)

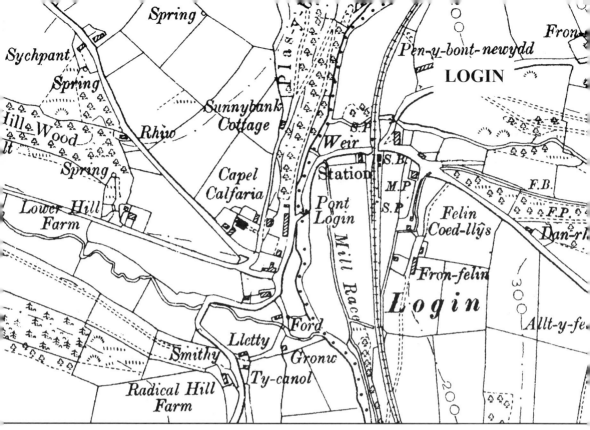

XIX.   The 1907 survey at 12ins to 1 mile shows the proximity of the Afon Taf to the line. It carries the dots of the parish boundary.

79.   The sign is failing in its final year of serving passengers. The single siding also closed then and the telephone pole is failing as well. (Lens of Sutton coll.)

80.   There was a staff of two in the 1930s and the substantial building became a home in the 1960s; it still stands. (Lens of Sutton coll.)

Login	1903	1913	1923	1933
Passenger tickets issued	4979	4559	5421	3846
Season tickets issued	*	*	10	35
Parcels forwarded	994	2859	10574	12898
General goods forwarded (tons)	90	40	70	19
Coal and coke received (tons)	346	297	258	145
Other minerals received (tons)	384	225	526	15
General goods received (tons)	198	183	468	200
Coal and Coke handled	-	10	40	36
Trucks of livestock handled	-	-	3	4

2085   2nd · SINGLE   SINGLE · 2nd   2085

LOGIN to

LOGIN   LOGIN
Llanglydwen   Llanglydwen

LLANGLYDWEN

(W)   6d.   FARE   6d.   (W)

For conditions see over   ...nditions see over

LLANGLYDWEN

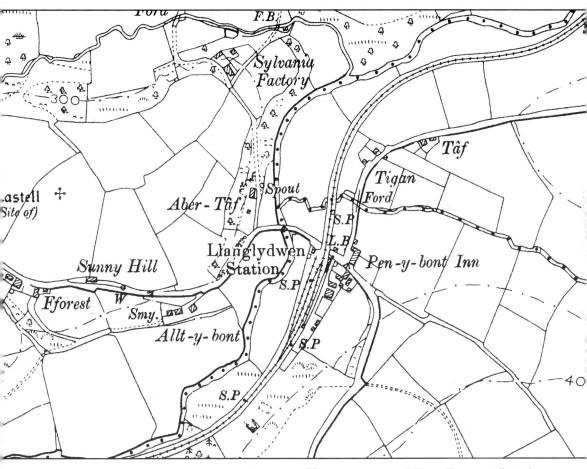

XX. Two tributaries join the Taf on this 12ins scale extract from 1907.

81. Most of our photographs were taken on 8th July 1958, this one including the photographer's parents. On the right is the parcels shed and the gents. Its water tank projects through the roof and is fed from the front gutter. This presumably was to reduce manual pumping from the river. (R.M.Casserley)

82.   The camera was turned about 90 degrees to record 0-6-0PT no. 1637 with the 6.15pm from Whitland. There were four men employed here in the 1930s. (R.M.Casserley)

83.   A stroll down the platform and a coal wagon comes into view, near the signalman who has the hoop in hand. Goods traffic was handled here until 27th May 1963 and the area continued in use as a coal yard. (R.M.Casserley)

84.	Having waited for the 5.45 from Cardigan to arrive behind 2-6-2T no. 4550, the signalman will have returned to his box to attend to the tablet machine. (R.M.Casserley)

85.	The box comes into view in this 1962 photograph. It had 16 levers and closed when passenger service ceased. The cottages were for railwaymen. (Lens of Sutton coll.)

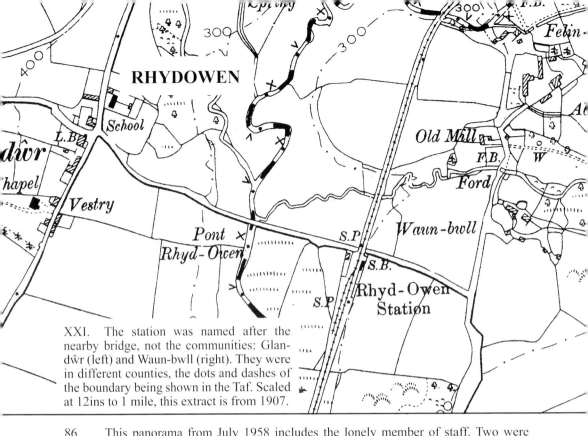

RHYDOWEN

XXI. The station was named after the nearby bridge, not the communities: Glan-dŵr (left) and Waun-bwll (right). They were in different counties, the dots and dashes of the boundary being shown in the Taf. Scaled at 12ins to 1 mile, this extract is from 1907.

86. This panorama from July 1958 includes the lonely member of staff. Two were listed in the 1930s, but they probably worked in overlapping shifts, this being a common practice. (R.M.Casserley)

87.　　This view in the other direction is shortly before total closure. The crews of subsequent freight trains had to work the gates themselves. No trace of the buildings remains. There had been a siding curving to the right beyond the crossing to Mr. Bishop's Penlan slate quarry in about 1880-86. (Lens of Sutton coll.)

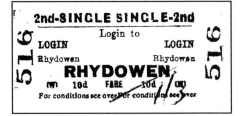

Rhydowen	1903	1913	1923	1933
Passenger tickets issued	3374	3760	3846	2121
Season tickets issued	*	*	12	6
Parcels forwarded	844	1713	2564	2088
General goods forwarded (tons)	206	139	88	47
Coal and coke received (tons)	218	123	225	146
Other minerals received (tons)	134	366	227	95
General goods received (tons)	546	418	791	451
Coal and Coke handled	5	-	42	56
Trucks of livestock handled	14	77	114	39

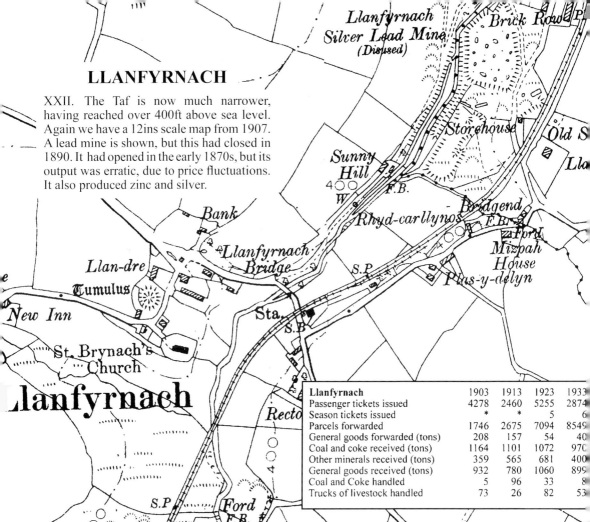

LLANFYRNACH

XXII. The Taf is now much narrower, having reached over 400ft above sea level. Again we have a 12ins scale map from 1907. A lead mine is shown, but this had closed in 1890. It had opened in the early 1870s, but its output was erratic, due to price fluctuations. It also produced zinc and silver.

Llanfyrnach	1903	1913	1923	1933
Passenger tickets issued	4278	2460	5255	2874
Season tickets issued	*	*	5	6
Parcels forwarded	1746	2675	7094	8549
General goods forwarded (tons)	208	157	54	40
Coal and coke received (tons)	1164	1101	1072	970
Other minerals received (tons)	359	565	681	400
General goods received (tons)	932	780	1060	899
Coal and Coke handled	5	96	33	8
Trucks of livestock handled	73	26	82	53

88.   We have the rare sight of a canopy on the branch; maybe it was due to the demands of a local landowner, rather than the higher rainfall here. Targets and lamps on the gates had not yet become a requirement. The box had seven levers and was in use as a ground frame from 1911until line closure. (Lens of Sutton coll.)

89.　　A 1958 record features the parcels sheds and a noteworthy way of economising in white paint. Again, there was a staff of two in the 1930s. The building became a dwelling. (R.M.Casserley)

90.　　The goods yard is seen in about 1962, along with the recently built store for bagged fertiliser. These white buildings appeared at countless rural stations in the 1950s. Freight ceased here with passenger service. (Lens of Sutton coll.)

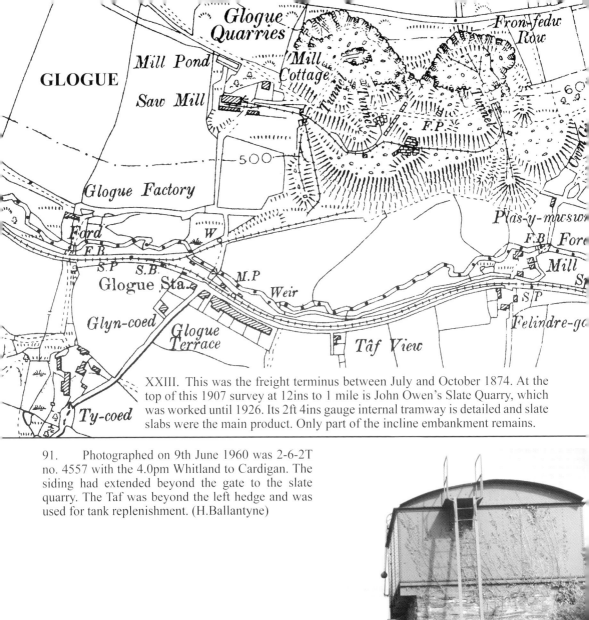

XXIII. This was the freight terminus between July and October 1874. At the top of this 1907 survey at 12ins to 1 mile is John Owen's Slate Quarry, which was worked until 1926. Its 2ft 4ins gauge internal tramway is detailed and slate slabs were the main product. Only part of the incline embankment remains.

91.   Photographed on 9th June 1960 was 2-6-2T no. 4557 with the 4.0pm Whitland to Cardigan. The siding had extended beyond the gate to the slate quarry. The Taf was beyond the left hedge and was used for tank replenishment. (H.Ballantyne)

92.   A train bound for Cardigan waits for the photographer on 21st August 1961. The water bag is in use and so he has no rush. (E.Wilmshurst)

93.   The entire platform is featured in this record from about 1962, along with the parcels shed. On the right is a fire-devil, which had to be kept alight on frosty nights to prevent the water tank and pipes from freezing. (Lens of Sutton coll.)

94.   The top of its chimney is evident as 2-6-2T no. 4558 takes water while working a train to Whitland, shortly before closure to passengers. Water was plentiful here, but not at the summit station. (Lens of Sutton coll.)

Glogue	1903	1913	1923	1933
Passenger tickets issued	4596	4093	5824	2585
Season tickets issued	*	*	-	9
Parcels forwarded	1235	1581	2090	2354
General goods forwarded (tons)	48	56	52	13
Coal and coke received (tons)	182	514	509	359
Other minerals received (tons)	64	76	326	30
General goods received (tons)	321	287	390	250
Coal and Coke handled	-	30	12	11
Trucks of livestock handled	-	-	-	-

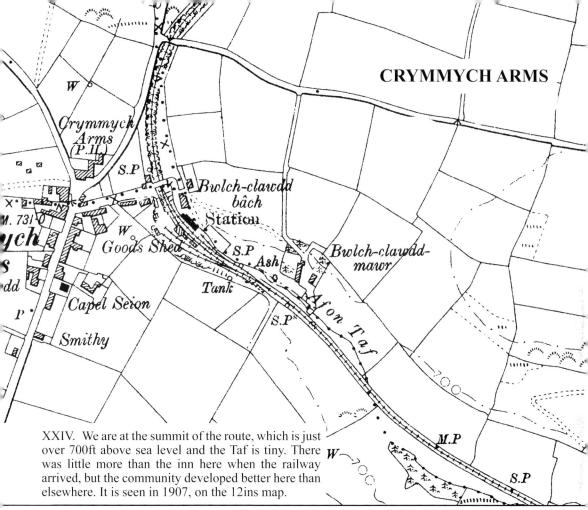

CRYMMYCH ARMS

XXIV. We are at the summit of the route, which is just over 700ft above sea level and the Taf is tiny. There was little more than the inn here when the railway arrived, but the community developed better here than elsewhere. It is seen in 1907, on the 12ins map.

95. This panorama from the south is probably on a market day, as cattle wagons are in profusion. Their white patches are due to lime used liberally as a hygiene measure. The market was on the last Tuesday of every month. (Lens of Sutton coll.)

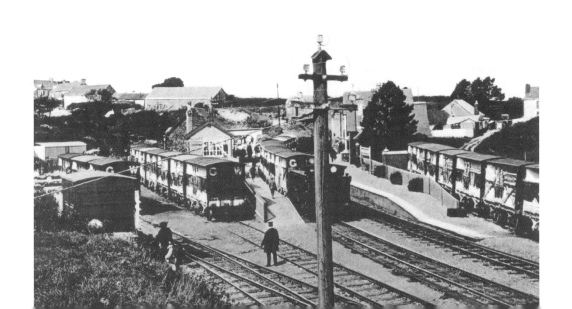

96.   A similar view from around 1920 has a more balanced selection of wagons, at a time when there were four employees. This dropped to three in the 1930s. The cattle pen is seen in part on the left. (Lens of Sutton coll.)

97.   The 5.45pm from Cardigan was headed by 2-6-2T no. 4550 on 8th July 1958. The adjacent platform and a new layout came in 1897. A refreshment room was run by the station master from 1876. (H.C.Casserley)

98.   Seen on the same day is 0-6-0PT no. 1637 with the 6.15pm Whitland to Cardigan. Near the goods shed is a fairly new Morris Commercial. (H.C.Casserley)

Crymmyeh Arms	1903	1913	1923	1933
Passenger tickets issued	8003	6879	6842	7819
Season tickets issued	*	*	10	6
Parcels forwarded	2707	4582	10497	8645
General goods forwarded (tons)	171	230	1506	198
Coal and coke received (tons)	2474	1899	1657	1598
Other minerals received (tons)	711	617	1147	1920
General goods received (tons)	1845	2028	3280	3104
Coal and Coke handled	119	262	575	886
Trucks of livestock handled	344	285	270	146

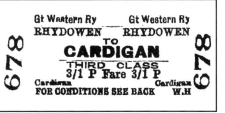

99.   The 4.0pm Whitland to Cardigan is seen on 9th June 1960, behind 2-6-2T no. 4557. Passengers used the crossing in the foreground, but only about one quarter of this train. (H.Ballantyne)

WHITLAND, CRYMMYCH ARMS and CARDIGAN
WEEK DAYS ONLY—(Second class only)

Mls		am	am	pm S	pm	pm S	pm E		Mls		am	am	pm	
	Whitland .. .. dep	6 20	11 35	3 40	4 0	5 13	6 18			Cardigan D .. .. dep	6 50	10 0	5 45	.
3¾	Llanfalteg Halt	6 31	11 45	3 50	4 10	5 24	6 29		3	Kilgerran Halt	6 59	10 9	5 54	...
6	Login Halt	6 41	11 55	4 0	4 20	5 34	6 39		6½	Boncath	7 14	10 23	6 9	...
8¾	Llanglydwen	6 53	12 7	4 12	4 32	5 47	6 57		11	Crymmych Arms	7 29	10 36	6 22	...
10¼	Rhydowen Halt	6 59	12 13	4 18	4 38	5 53	7 3		13¼	Glogue Halt	7 40	10 46	6 33	...
12¾	Llanfyrnach	7 8	12 22	4 26	4 46	6 2	7 12		14½	Llanfyrnach	7 47	10 52	6 40	...
14	Glogue Halt	7 19	12 30	4 34	4 54	6 10	7 20		17¼	Rhydowen Halt	7 56	11 1	6 49	...
16½	Crymmych Arms	7 33	12 40	4 44	5 4	6 23	7 30		18½	Llanglydwen	8 2	11 8	6 56	...
21	Boncath	7 55	12 53	4 57	5 17	6 36	7 43		21½	Login Halt	8 14	11 19	7 6	...
24¼	Kilgerran Halt	8 5	1 3	5 7	5 27	6 46	7 53		23½	Llanfalteg Halt	8 24	11 29	7 16	...
27½	Cardigan D .. arr	8 14	1 12	5 16	5 36	6 55	8 2		27½	Whitland .. .. arr	8 35	11 40	7 29	.

D Station for Gwbert-on-Sea (3¼ miles)
E Except Saturdays
S Saturdays only

June 1962 - The final timetable.

2nd—SINGLE SINGLE—2nd
Rhydowen to
Rhydowen   Rhydowen
Llanglydwen   Llanglydwen
LLANGLYDWEN
(W) 4d Fare 4d (W)
For conditions see over For conditions see over
1912 1912

Gt. Western Ry.   Gt. Western Ry.
PRIVILEGE TICKET   PRIVILEGE TICKET
Llanglydwen to   RHYDOWEN to
RHYDOWEN   **LLANGLYDWEN**
THIRD CLASS   THIRD CLASS
Fare 3d. N   Fare 3d. N
A.I. See back   A.I. See back
082 082

100.   We finish with two views from 20th June 1962. The signal box of 1897 had 23 levers and lasted until 27th May 1963. This was the only station on the branch to have a station master, he being responsible for the others. (R.G.Nelson/R.S.Carpenter)

101.   The yard continued to receive coal by road until 26th October 1964 and was later adapted to become a market. The bridge from which this picture was taken gave access to the main station building, left. (R.G.Nelson/R.S.Carpenter)

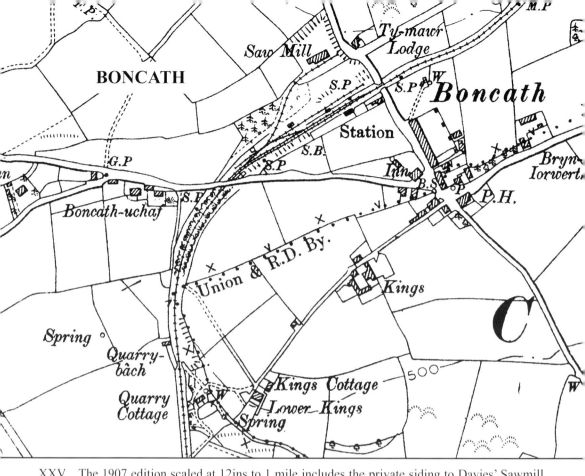

XXV.   The 1907 edition scaled at 12ins to 1 mile includes the private siding to Davies' Sawmill and evidence of a small quarry. It had no siding.

102.   A view towards Cardigan on 8th July 1958 features the main building and the parcels shed. The staff had numbered two for most of the 1930s. (H.C.Casserley)

103.   Looking in the other direction in June 1962, we see the goods loop and its ringed signal. These had been added in 1941, when the other loop was lengthened. The building became a dwelling. (B.W.L.Brooksbank)

104.   We can enjoy two photographs from 20th June 1962. This features one of the bogie ventilated vans used for overnight fruit and vegetable traffic. One of the lower ventilators has its shutter missing. (R.G.Nelson/R.S.Carpenter)

105.   The signal box had 17 levers and was in use from 1886 until 1962. There was once a heavy
traffic in rabbits (dead) from this station. Ventilated vans would have been ideal. Freight traffic
ceased on 27th May 1963, but the goods shed was already derelict. (R.G.Nelson/R.S.Carpenter)

Boncath	1903	1913	1923	1933
Passenger tickets issued	7470	7208	7237	1266
Season tickets issued	*	*	56	5
Parcels forwarded	4261	5456	8015	11412
General goods forwarded (tons)	885	1744	965	816
Coal and coke received (tons)	1407	1471	882	1281
Other minerals received (tons)	2222	1277	792	1449
General goods received (tons)	1245	2066	1576	845
Coal and Coke handled	812	856	456	238
Trucks of livestock handled	105	176	154	103

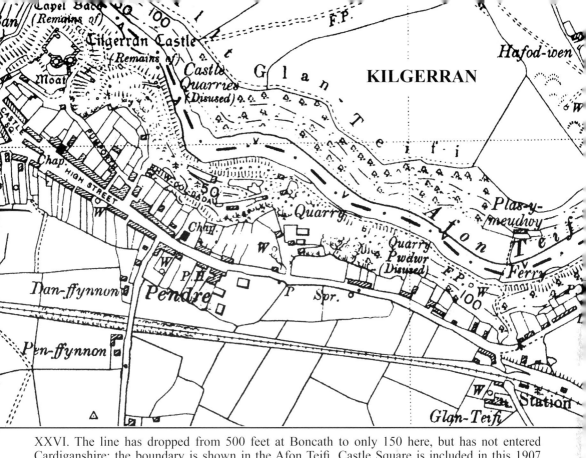

XXVI. The line has dropped from 500 feet at Boncath to only 150 here, but has not entered Cardiganshire; the boundary is shown in the Afon Teifi. Castle Square is included in this 1907 extract, scaled at 12ins to 1 mile.

106.   Few postcards feature cranes in action; this one was rated at 5-tons and is hand worked. Also note the cart being unloaded onto the platform. The village is Cilgerran (C is always hard in Wales), but the railways have insisted on a K. (Lens of Sutton coll.)

Kilgerran	1903	1913	1923	1933
Passenger tickets issued	10246	9727	8432	1453
Season tickets issued	*	*	84	-
Parcels forwarded	2333	4429	2724	3259
General goods forwarded (tons)	310	1200	1257	1165
Coal and coke received (tons)	1751	1494	687	713
Other minerals received (tons)	424	569	880	575
General goods received (tons)	297	613	380	346
Coal and Coke handled	172	483	616	301
Trucks of livestock handled	53	56	15	8

107.   On the right is the passenger entrance and centre is a wooden platform for the ground frame. There had been a signal box until about 1899. This and the next two photographs are from 1958. (H.C.Casserley)

108.   The small building is seen from a train bound for Cardigan, but it has since vanished. The population was 1033 in 1901 and 815 in 1961. (H.C.Casserley)

109.   Bound for Cardigan is 2-6-2T no. 5549. Goods traffic continued here until 27th March 1963, although staffing had ceased on 10th September 1956. The goods shed remained standing long after and the term "Halt" was applied. (D.K.Jones coll.)

CARDIGAN

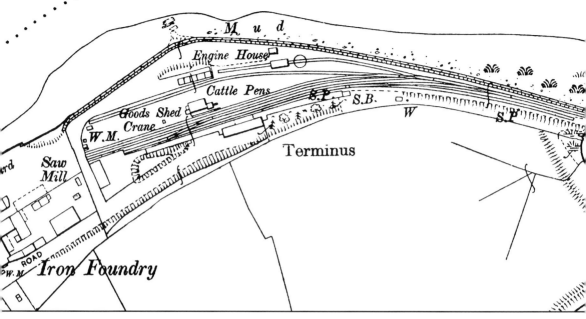

XXVII. The 1911 edition details a layout which appears to have never altered. The river is along the top border, and the town is on its other bank. Its population was 3510 in 1901 and 3740 in 1961.

110. This Edwardian postcard view is looking west, the unoccupied line being the run-round loop. The staff numbered 11 or 12 in the 1930s. Ship building had declined locally, as had maritime traffic, in the 19th century. (Lens of Sutton coll.)

111.   The approach road was inclined upwards away from the station and is occupied by the photographer's Hillman 10 on 8th July 1958. On the left is a recent Morris Oxford. (H.C.Casserley)

112.   Minutes later, we see 2-6-2T no. 4550 at the west end of the platform. The signal box had a 12-lever frame and was in use until the end of passenger services. (H.C.Casserley)

113.   Holiday luggage and boxes predominate following the arrival of 2-6-2T no. 4557 with the 4.00pm from Whitland on 9th June 1960. A late addition was the extension to the roof over the goods platform. (H.Ballantyne)

Cardigan	1903	1913	1923	1933
Passenger tickets issued	18538	18269	15818	3017
Season tickets issued	*	*	8	8
Parcels forwarded	19760	29127	30452	35314
General goods forwarded (tons)	1722	1966	1657	574
Coal and coke received (tons)	4388	4165	2742	5256
Other minerals received (tons)	1387	1843	5980	4535
General goods received (tons)	3447	5324	8503	8068
Coal and Coke handled	985	2736	5277	2298
Trucks of livestock handled	295	344	500	406

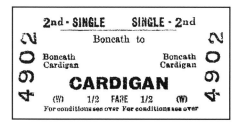

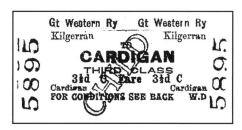

114.   Waiting to depart with the 5.45pm on 21st August 1961 is 2-6-2T no. 5549. The gardens welcomed arriving passengers and were well kept to the end. (E.Wilmshurst)

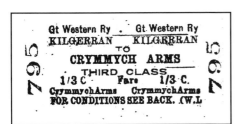

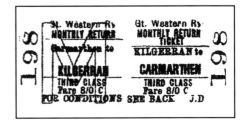

July 1927

Miles	Down.	Week Days only.				Miles	Up.	Week Days only.			
		mrn	mrn	aft	aft			mrn	mrn	aft	aft
	Whitland ....dep.	6 5	1040	2 30	6 15		Cardigan........dep.	7 0	10 5	1235	5 35
3¼	Llanfalteg	6 15	1050	2 40	6 25	3	Kilgerran	7 9	10 14	1244	5 48
6	Login	6 25	11 0	2 50	6 35	6½	Boncath	7 22	10 27	1257	6 0
8½	Llanglydwen	6 36	1113	3 1	6 47	11	Crymmych Arms....	7 36	10 41	1 11	6 14
10½	Rhydowen............	6 43	1119	3 8	6 53	13½	Glogue	7 46	10 51	1 21	6 24
12½	Llanfyrnach	6 51	1128	3 16	7 2	14½	Llanfynach	7 52	10 57	1 27	6 30
14	Glogue	6 58	1135	3 23	7 9	17½	Rhydowen..........	8 0	11 5	1 36	6 38
16½	Crymmych Arms	7 7	1144	3 32	7 18	18½	Llanglydwen	8 7	11 13	1 42	6 46
21	Boncath	7 22	1159	3 47	7 33	21½	Login	8 19	11 24	1 53	6 57
24½	Kilgerran	7 33	1210	3 58	7 44	23½	Llanfalteg	8 33	11 34	2 3	7 7
27½	**Cardigan D** ...... arr.	7 41	1218	4 6	7 52	27½	**Whitland** 62, 67, 97 arr.	8 42	11 43	2 12	7 16

WHITLAND, CRYMMYCH ARMS, and CARDIGAN.

D Station for Gwbert-on-Sea (3½ miles) and St. Dogmells (1¼ miles).

115.   It is September 1961 and 2-6-2T no. 5549 has just arrived. BR offered a service called "Passengers Luggage in Advance", which ensured your holiday garments arrived at your accommodation before you did. (D.K.Jones coll.)

↓ 116. A fine panorama from 20th June 1962 includes the lofty crane, capable of lifting six tons, and a still busy goods yard. The right post contained a hoist for raising a Tilley lamp. (R.G.Nelson /R.S.Carpenter)

117.   The view in the other direction on the same day includes the Afon Teifi, with a water column nearby. The despondent staff had given up collecting litter from the track, as the end was nigh. (R.G.Nelson/R.S.Carpenter)

118. Three photographs from the same occasion complete our survey of the facilities. The shed was allocated one 2-6-2T and one 0-6-0PT back in 1947. The turntable was 23ft 6ins long, just large enough for a small 0-6-0PT. (R.G.Nelson/R.S.Carpenter)

→ 119. The BR shed code was sub to 87H, but only basic items were provided. The station building became offices for an agricultural equipment supplier, but the engine shed was demolished. (R.G.Nelson/R.S.Carpenter)

→ 120. The engine shed was closed with the end of passenger service in September 1962, it having opened in 1885. The closure of Llanfalteg shed in 1897, made it sole provider on the branch. Goods traffic ceased on 27th May 1963, but the shed remained standing, a memorial to earlier enterprise. (R.G.Nelson/R.S.Carpenter)

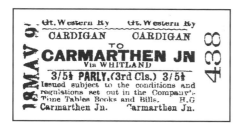

Middleton Press

EVOLVING THE ULTIMATE RAIL ENCYCLOPEDIA

Easebourne Lane, Midhurst, West Sussex.
GU29 9AZ   Tel:01730 813169
www.middletonpress.co.uk email:info@middletonpress.co.uk
A-978 0 906520 B-978 1 873793 C- 978 1 901706 D-978 1 904474
E - 978 1 906008   F - 978 1 908174

All titles listed below were in print at time of publication - please check current availability by looking at our website - **www.middletonpress.co.uk** or by requesting a Brochure which includes our *LATEST* RAILWAY TITLES also our TRAMWAY, TROLLEYBUS, MILITARY and COASTAL series